From Interior Design Intern To Employee: How to Be a "Keeper"

Including Tips From Those Who Hire

By Jeanette H. Simpson, ASID
KidSpace Interiors

www.InternToEmployee.com
May 2009

From Interior Design Intern to Employee:
How to Be a "Keeper"
Including Tips from Those Who Hire
(First Edition)

Simpson, Jeanette H.
    From interior design intern to employee : how to be a "keeper" : including tips from those who hire / Jeanette H. Simpson, ASID.
    120 pgs.

    ISBN 978-0-557-07044-2 (6 x 9 pbk)

Cover design by Jeanette Simpson
Cover Photo by Tom Simpson
            Focal-Point Photography, www.focal-pointphoto.com

This book is available at special quantity discounts to use for educational purposes. Please email sales@interntoemployee.com to order or for more information.

To Tom,
thank you
for believing
in me.

Acknowledgements

When spending time on any important project, be it for a class, a client or just for personal fulfillment, there are often many hours spent working during the early morning before the sun has risen or late into the evening or sometimes even pulling an all-nighter.

During a project, you tend to have a one-track mind focusing all your attention on the task at hand and ignoring those around you, especially when you have a deadline. Sometimes you are consumed with the drive to completion.

There were times during this project that I did all of these things. Well, maybe not the all-nighter but I did wake up with ideas running through my mind at all hours of the night!

I have long dreamed of writing this book, but with my busy work and family schedules, it was not a priority. As my husband encouraged me to write this book, I continued to dismiss the idea. In face, I dismissed it for a full year. It was only after his continual encouragement that I decided to put my thoughts and experiences to paper.

To those interns, entry-level designers and architects who unknowingly assisted by taking part in the studies out of which this project grew, thank you for helping to confirm that the need for this book was real.

To those educators in the university interior design departments scattered across the country, thank you for your participation in the study. Your replies provided valuable insight pertaining to students' fears as well as their needs in finding employment.

To those professional interior designers who participated, your candor was invaluable. Thank you for taking time out of your busy schedules to take part in the study. Your replies helped validate my thoughts on interns and related hiring issues.

To my family, friends and fellow design professionals who proofread and offered comments, thank you for taking the time to read the manuscript. Having new sets of "eyes" reviewing from a different viewpoint has been very beneficial.

To my (late) Aunt Doris who inspired me to become a designer through her many tours of the beautiful homes and estates each time we visited her in Atlanta and Sarasota, I am grateful and indebted. She was the beginning source of my love for architecture and design.

To my parents who encouraged me to get my education, paid my college tuition and for all my many design supplies, thank you for instilling in me throughout my life the belief that I could accomplish anything.

To my children for being my research models as I gained experience in seeing what children need in their development and for being my inspiration to open KidSpace Interiors, thank you for your love and support as I was away from home working to gain the experience necessary to obtain my design license.

To Tom, my husband, my sweetheart and the one who calmed my fears when my confidence was low, encouraged me to get the experience I needed and took care of the family while I worked, thank you for providing quiet time while I studied for my NCIDQ licensing exam and for enduring my endless looking around at furniture and finishes everywhere we go. Most of all, thank you for telling me I could write this book and believing in me.

To those who read *From Interior Design Intern to Employee: How to Be a "Keeper"*, may the information herein be of great benefit to you in your transition from the life of a college student to the world of work. May you enjoy the exciting field of interior design and have great success throughout your professional career.

Contents

Chapter 1:
Introduction

You have burned the midnight oil designing spaces, drawing plans, creating models and assembling presentation boards. You have spent hours digging for fabric samples, furniture photos and finish materials. There are times you wish college would never end. Other times you can hardly wait to start working on actual projects.

But in the whirlwind of projects and presentations, did you take time to prepare yourself for those challenges that you will encounter as an entry-level designer? Do you know what it takes to secure the position you want or do you even know in which segment of the industry you want to work?

Working as an intern is the best way to try out a new job without making a permanent commitment. An internship is short-term work experience where you will be immersed in the world of design under the guidance of a mentor. The process of finding an internship and getting hired is similar to what it takes to get hired into a career position.

There is a lot of information circulating about internships and about how to find the right one, what to do when you get it and what to do when it is over. The information is usually very generic in nature and not aimed specifically at helping future design professionals.

The information in this book is different. It is written with interior design students in mind and covers areas specific to the design industry. Then after addressing this information, it goes one step further and explains the steps to take to secure a career position after the internship is over. In short, this book shows you how to be a "keeper".

You may be wondering why a book specifically about interior design internships would even need to be written. There are several reasons but the most notable ones are:

1) There is a real gap between the academic world and the design industry. What an entry-level designer has learned in school and the skillsets he or she brings to the table is far from the only thing a prospective employer is looking for. An interior designer is required to know a great deal about many things, from design to constructability, furniture and finish selection to care and maintenance, space planning to code requirements, as well as marketing and procurement.

Besides these fundamental aspects of interior design, there are certain skills that can only be developed through experience. Employers know that the best teacher for the time management, interpersonal communication and fundamental business skills required in the design business is real world experience.

2) The transition from full-time education to full-time employment can be overwhelming. As a student, you hope you have learned what is essential to fulfill employer expectations

but without an internship, you have no way of knowing whether you have obtained the skills that will be required of you.

3) At times a designer's workload can be heavy and an extra hand is always welcomed, especially during weeks when deadlines are looming. For some firms, the extra hand can be an entry-level designer but their assistance ranges from invaluable to...well, let's say not so great.

4) For an employer, hiring someone right out of school can be somewhat daunting. Hiring someone right out of school *who has had an internship* makes the task much easier. Knowing an applicant has begun developing work related skills makes the selection process less complicated.

In my experience with interns, I have seen a need for bridging the gap between what an intern expects from an internship and what an employer actually requires. The need to bridge this gap provided the foundation for my research and led me to survey two separate groups of professionals: interior design educators and interior design professionals.

Educators were asked what they felt you, the student, needed most out of a book designed to help you prepare for an internship. The educators replied that tips from those who hire interns and information about how to actually get an internship would be the most helpful. Also high on the educators' list of things you needed to know before interning was tips on things to do and not do during an internship.

Design professionals were asked what employers were hoping to get from an intern. Their survey replies included what they look for when hiring an intern, giving added emphasis to skills and abilities an employer needs and expects an intern to know. Also covered were problem areas that continue to surface causing some students to not receive a job offer.

This book has covered the concerns of both the educators and designers. Thrown in with all the tips they offered are many questions for you to answer during your internship preparation. The question topics range from personal to design to business to social skills and abilities. Some in depth self-reflection will be necessary on your part in order for you to make best use of the advice given.

I have written this book to help not only the industry and future employers find the best candidate to fill a position, but to help you become that best candidate. If followed, this information will arm you with more than the essentials enabling you to develop into the best intern and subsequently upon graduation, become a welcome, valuable full-time addition to any company within the design industry.

Chapter 2:
Why Intern?

Since most interior design schools require an internship as part of their curriculum, you may not have a choice on whether to intern or not. Most schools already have a program set up however, if yours does not have an internship program, create your own. More information about how to do this will be given in the next chapter.

There are many more reasons to intern than to not and the benefits far out-weigh the disadvantages. Listed here are some of the top reasons to intern.

25 Ways You Can Benefit from an Internship

- Earn credit and money simultaneously.

- Apply classroom education by testing what you have learned.

- Experience firsthand things you cannot learn in the classroom.

- Able to test and refine knowledge as you begin to develop confidence and competencies in professional skills.

- College curriculum becomes more meaningful as your internship assignments relate to course material in turn helping you see the value of your class lessons.

- Compare what you now know to what you actually need to know.

- Helps you learn more about yourself, your skills and aspirations.

- Validates your career direction is correct – before you finish and realize you do not really like the industry.

- Helps you to navigate everyday work challenges such as getting along with coworkers, dealing with office politics, and making difficult decisions.

- Develop skills necessary for any work environment including verbal and written communication, interpersonal skills, teamwork, time management and goal setting.

- Gives you exposure to new ideas and different ways of thinking.

- Observe challenges inherent in making decisions in complex situations.

- Assists you in developing a personal set of professional values, ethics and standards.

- Inside knowledge and insight into industry.

- Helps you make transition from student to professional as you begin to think like a professional instead of a student.

- Network as you meet and connect with others in the field, which often provides leads on other workplaces that might be hiring.

- Provides personal references for future employers from a business associate rather than a family friend.

- Practice the art of finding and getting a job.

- Opportunity to build your resume.

- Offers the experience employers look for.

- Increases your credibility and marketability after graduation.

- Gives you a competitive advantage over other applicants.

- Assures you have meaningful experiences to discuss during job interviews.

- Helps you command a higher starting salary – grads that have had internships generally are paid more.

- Most graduates begin job search **after** graduation – after stress of finals, etc. An internship provides the opportunity to begin thinking about the future, making contacts and gathering information **before** graduation.

How Employers Benefit from Internships

Internships are one of the best ways for college students to gain valuable hands-on or "real world" experience that employers are demanding. Some employers overwhelmingly point to internship experience as the most important factor they consider when hiring.

Why? You will not need as much training and handholding as a new employee. Because you have already received some basic training, your ramp up to speed is accelerated when you already have some experience.

Employers can also draw some important conclusions about you if you have participated in at least one internship: you are still interested in design and are serious about the industry, you probably have the right stuff, and have a high level of commitment. Employers who hire people with internship experience can be sure they are hiring people who know they want to be in their particular profession.

One of my favorite quotes about internships points out their importance as seen through an employer's eyes:

> *"Measuring an internship-exposed student against a noninternship-exposed student can best be compared to the difference between a roll of film and a photograph. Both started out the same way – with potential. The difference is in the development." (Errica Rivera)*

Top Reasons Why Designers Do NOT Hire Interns

Still, knowing how beneficial internships can be in providing students with experience and training, why do some designers choose to not hire interns? We asked designers around the USA and quoted here are some of their reasons.

- "Interns do not understand that an internship is more than just a break time job."
- "We get more work out of an intern architect than interiors intern."
- "Unrealistic expectations – they think they should get to design – don't know enough."

- "Often, the effort required to educate and train interns out-weighs the productivity they are able to contribute."
- "Too busy to train and check work."
- "Work received is ¼ of time invested in the intern."
- "Company is too small to need help - not enough workload to justify hiring an intern."
- "Have not found interns with adequate skills."
- "Many interns have chip on their shoulder and have little experience."
- "Interns do not have enough office skills – realistically more office work is done than design."
- "Have to fit class schedule into design firm workday. "

Although this list shows the negative traits demonstrated by some interns, learn from their mistakes. Rewrite each comment to read as a positive statement then focus on what you *should* do. Make sure these negative comments do not describe you. If they do describe you, change it now! Be one of the reasons they are glad they hired an intern.

Now that you know *why* you should intern and why many designers do not hire interns, your next move is finding out *how* to find and get an internship.

Chapter 3:
How to Find and Get an Internship

You have almost completed your education – now it is time to put your knowledge and skills to the test as an intern. But how do you find an internship? When do start your search and where do you look? What should you look for in an internship program?

What are employers looking for when they interview? Who can you ask for help and whom do you need to contact to apply for a job? What if a design firm you would really like to work for does not have an internship program?

The information in this chapter will answer many of these questions but it will also encourage you to do an in-depth personal assessment that will be needed for you to answer the rest. You will also have to do some advance preparation before you begin your internship search.

As was mentioned earlier, completing an internship is a major step toward getting hired full-time after graduation. However, before you can even start dreaming about your first design job, you need to prepare for your first internship and think about what you want from that experience.

Prepare Before the Search Begins

There are four key areas you need to focus on during the preparation process: deciding what you want to accomplish, assessing personal traits and work skills, researching industry segments that interest you and developing your resume and portfolio.

Decide What You Want to Accomplish:

Think about the way you work best by seriously pondering the following questions. Which do you value most: flexibility, creativity or coworker interaction? Do you want to learn a specific skill or just beef-up your resume? Do you need cash as an incentive or can you work for free or next to nothing? Does your school have specific internship requirements you need to meet prior to graduation?

Before starting the search for an internship, you will need to answer these questions. Use your answers to help you create a checklist of skills you hope to learn, people you want to meet, types of projects you would like to work on, etc. Later, you can check these items off the list as the internship progresses to ensure that you are making the most of your experience and meeting any school requirements. Also, during your search and subsequent interviews, you will sound more informed and focused if you can describe to potential employers exactly what kind of experience you want.

Chart your course, but be realistic. You may not be able to accomplish all of your goals during an internship. However, statistics show that those with written goals, which are reviewed daily, have a higher level of achievement and success, so plan ahead for success! Deciding what you want is the first step.

Assess Your Personality and Skills

Next, take a good, long look at yourself and assess your motives. Take into account your strengths, weaknesses, affinities and expectations. Be honest with yourself! What can you offer an employer *right now*? What improvements do you need to make?

Look at the list below and assess how well do you do in the following areas:

Personality Traits –

- Cheerful, happy demeanor
- Always pleasant
- Friendly and gets along well with others
- Positive "can do" attitude
- Perseveres through difficulties
- Enthusiastic with high energy level
- Mature, responsible and dependable
- Honest and trustworthy
- Able to maintain confidences
- High level of professional ethics and standards
- Poised and confident
- Dedicated and committed
- Observant and inquisitive
- Flexible, versatile and open-minded

- Humble and thoughtful of others
- Does not gossip or speak negatively of others

Work ethic –

- Willing and eager to learn, teachable
- Willing to do anything, fearless, not shy or timid
- Willing to work hard
- Self-starter, go-getter, has initiative
- Able to multi-task
- Able to work with limited assistance
- Organized and prepared
- Accurate and attentive to details
- Able to focus, attentive to others when needed
- Interested in all aspects of profession, not just designing
- Able to manage time efficiently, complete assignments quickly
- Reliable, punctual, dependable
- Not a clock watcher

Design Skills -

- Talented with passion for the profession
- Excellent color sense
- Good presentation skills and color board prep
- Good drawing and freehand sketching ability
- Good understanding of furniture and fabrics
- Good understanding of how to resource materials
- Able to think "outside the box"
- AutoCAD or REVIT, Studio IT, Photoshop familiarity

Office Skills –

- Office or retail experience

- Good telephone etiquette and language skills

- Good grammar and writing skills

- Familiar with basic office programs such as Word, Excel, etc.

- Computer hardware and software knowledge

- Excellent computer skills

People Skills –

- Well-mannered

- Good listener (incredibly important!)

- Good verbal communication

- Team player

- Easy speaking manner

- Problem solving skills

- Able to think on your feet

How well do you rate? Are there areas for improvement? You should begin improving personal traits and skills immediately. Do not wait until you start your internship (or graduate) before making adjustments. Now is your time to prepare.

Also, it is a good idea to ask for feedback from your family, friends and professors. You might even create a checklist from the list given above and use it for gathering and recording their feedback.

Research the Industry Segment that Interests You

If you have completed the first step, you have already decided what you want to do. However, at this point you may not know which segment of the industry you prefer. Answering these questions will you give added direction during your internship search.

Do you want to work in an interior design firm or a design department within an architectural firm? Would you be interested in space planning for a furniture or kitchen showroom? What about interning with a design/build business? Have you thought of working within a design department of a large corporation or retail business? Do you want to intern locally or in another location?

Do you want to do residential or commercial design? Are you interested in specialty areas such as healthcare, hospitality, corporate, retail or institutional design? Have you thought about government work? Do you eventually want to become a licensed professional?

Use your answers to these questions and begin to compile a list of company types or areas of specialty that interest you. Use the Internet to learn more about each industry segment, and then narrow your choices to the ones that may offer what you are looking for in a professional experience. You can also talk to professionals already working in these various areas to get opinions about their area of specialty.

Be sure to bookmark websites of interesting companies you find while researching so you can return later to check the employment opportunities listed.

Develop Your Resume' and Portfolio

You may be required to provide a resume' and portfolio when you apply for an internship, just as you would for an entry-level position. Even though these will not be as complete as they will be when you graduate, you should have all your documents ready, including a cover letter and references.

Be sure your portfolio includes drawings as well as examples of your design capability. These should be your work only, not those which include your associates' work. Also, providing your portfolio on a disk may seem to be a great idea but it is best to bring a small sampling of boards instead. Your interviewer should not have to access a computer during an interview to view your work.

Replies to the study ranked résumé's and portfolios in the middle of the road in importance to employers. They understand most of your portfolio is schoolwork. During the interview process, emphasis will be placed more on your character and abilities and less on how beautiful your student projects were. Many interns have nice looking portfolios. Employers are more interested in finding out about your character and work ethic.

Find and Get the Internship You Want

Now that you have gotten yourself prepared, decided what you want to accomplish, made a list of company types that interest you and prepared your documents, it is time to find the perfect internship for you!

Finding the internship you want will take some time and effort on your part. Be proactive. Do not wait for employers to come to campus. *You* need to find *them*. Many smaller or less structured companies do not recruit on campus.

As the whole process can be somewhat overwhelming, let's break it down into more manageable parts: when to look, where to look, what to look for, who to contact, and how to apply, followed by interview tips and after the interview follow-up.

When to Look

You should begin your research no later than two semesters prior to the term you would like to intern. The earlier you begin, the more time you will be able to spend on your search and have a better chance of finding what you want. You will also beat the last minute rush to get a job. It is never too early to begin your search!

If your internship is a class for credit, you may be required to intern during a specific semester or quarter as determined by your course curriculum. If not, you may schedule anytime during the year. Some company internships are typically available only during summer while others are offered during the school year.

Where to Look

While there are many apparent places to search, the list below will provide you with not only the obvious, it will also include resources beyond. Exhaust each one in your pursuit for the best internship. Be sure to consider smaller companies in your search, as there may be more opportunities and less competition. Smaller companies may also be able to provide a broader range of responsibilities.

Networking Sources

- Networking is the best way to land a job simply because you come with a built-in recommendation from a trusted friend.

- Talk to family members, former employers, friends and their parents. Tell everyone you know you are looking for an interior design internship. They may have a lead you do not know about.

- Word of mouth from others in the industry such as manufacturer's reps who have visited your classroom can lead to opportunities.

- Classmates may know of someone who is leaving an internship and the company is looking to find a replacement.

- Call designer showrooms. They may know of firms looking for assistance or need assistance themselves.

Associations for Design Professionals

- Search professional associations (such as ASID, IIDA, NKBA) job bank listings, keyword search - Intern

- Association publications may offer information on internship programs that are not widely advertised.

- Research professional publications for names of companies or designers you would be interested in working for.

- Attend functions hosted by local design organizations and get to know the local designers. This is a great way to learn as well as network for a job.

School Interior Design Department

- Your design department may have listings of available internships or ongoing relationships with specific companies.

- Talk to faculty members about contacts they may have with outside organizations or internships they know about.

31

School Career Services Office

- Your school may have an internship coordinator to assist you in your search and completion of applications.
- While career services assistance is usually school wide, they may also have listings of internships for interior designers. You don't know until you check!

Alumni Office

- The alumni office may maintain a database of job placement opportunities for students as well as graduates.
- School alumni can be a great source for finding internships. They may offer openings within their firms or know of available positions.

Internet Websites

- Start with sites that let you search specifically for interior design internships and then expand to other sites. (See Appendix D at the end of this book for helpful links.)
- Keyword search intern, internship or entry level
- If you have made the list of companies you are interested in, check the career section of their company website for job listings.

Internship and Career Fairs

- Go to the career fairs offered on campus, especially if you are enrolled at a school specializing in design. You never know what will turn up when networking with recruiters!

- When you go, it is <u>imperative</u> you dress like you would for an interview. You may be the only one who does so you will really stand out.
- Check with local temp agencies to see if they have any listings for design interns.

Books and Periodicals

- Local newspaper classifieds may have internship listings if you are in a larger metro area. Do a keyword search on their website. Advertised opportunities are typically established programs with more formal application processes.
- Local and school resource libraries have internship directories in the reference section. Check these for design specific listings.
- Trade magazines often publish information about internship programs.
- Remember to check the Yellow Pages, on and offline for listings of companies to call.

Cold Contact

- If none of these resources work, take the list of companies you have identified and start sending letters of inquiry with a follow-up call.

What to Look For

Internships vary widely in the amount of compensation given, credit offered, hours available and schedule you are required to keep, as well as, the amount of learning and supervision you receive. Use the following criteria to evaluate a potential internship:

- *Credit vs. Non-credit* – Most design curriculums require an internship prior to graduation and provide credit when completed as required. There may be more restrictions on the type and amount of work based on your program so keep this in mind during your search. If necessary for you to receive credit, be sure to obtain approval of your department prior to accepting a position.

  If you are not required to complete an internship for credit, do one anyway. The experience you obtain is worth far more than the credit you would receive.

- *Mentor-led vs. Self-directed* – If your school requires an internship, chances are you will have an academic advisor you are required to report to while working as an intern. The school may also encourage open communication between your supervisor and the faculty coordinator regarding your performance. Together, they may serve as mentors to track your progress.

  Some companies will hire interns but not provide a specific mentor or supervisor to see you achieve your goals, or the one assigned may be lax in supervision. In this case, it will be up to you to track your progress and ask for assignments that will help you meet your requirements.

- *Term vs. Summer* – Most design school internships are set up as an off-campus course that can be taken any term during the school year. You will need to look at your particular schedule for graduation and plan accordingly.

Also, any summer job you have can give you extra experience beyond your graduation requirements, whether for credit or not. Each job between terms should be geared toward enlarging your experience in the design industry.

- *Part-time vs. Full-time* – Your school may have a set number of hours you need to work during your internship to meet program requirements, which may determine whether you need to work full or part-time. Be sure to verify this with potential employers so they schedule you accordingly as some companies only offer part-time internships.

  You may have the opportunity to work part-time during the school year or may need to do so for financial reasons. Some school programs prefer you avoid working during the school year due to heavy project workloads. This is something you will have to evaluate based on need and your ability to handle school and work at the same time.

  Sometimes you may need to take a break from school and refocus or even replenish your financial coffers. A full-time internship during a semester off can help realign your career goals while providing a break and also give you much needed experience.

- *Paid vs. Unpaid* - Fortunately most design firms feel interns should be paid for their work, however there are some who will allow students to run errands without pay to just be in the office and experience the day-to-day operation. Unpaid interns are usually only there for a few hours each week for the purpose of observation.

Paid internships tend to be more professional as the employer wants to get their money's worth from you. It will most likely be minimum wage but the connections you make and training you receive are where your value will be found.

Who to Contact

In your research of organizations, call ahead and find out who makes the hiring decision. Find out who places interns and whom the right person is to contact. Speaking directly with the decision maker is always best but they may not be easily accessible.

Sometimes, alumni and students who have completed internships can get "your foot in the door" and introduce you to the right person. This is a great form of networking!

As you meet people at design events, talk to them about internships. They may have a position open or know of someone else who does and put you in contact with the right person.

How to Apply

Gather all of your previously prepared documents and make sure you proofread them carefully! This is your first introduction to a potential employer and your first chance to impress them. If you have sloppy spelling, capitalization and grammar, they might think your work will have the same problems and dismiss you immediately.

Your cover letter should be designed to draw an employer in, making them want to get the details from your resume'. It should highlight the parts of your experience specific to the internship they are offering. Be prepared to submit any additional information as well when requested.

Next, based on your prior research, choose your target companies. Contact first by mail, sending letters of inquiry then follow-up with a telephone call about a week later. You may also visit employers in your geographic area of interest to inquire if they offer internship opportunities. As you receive information, eliminate organizations based on their capacity to provide the experience you want.

Email may be quicker method of delivery for your letter, but chances are it will be considered spam. Most companies have spam blockers in place so your letter might not even reach your target. You may send your resume' by email, or fax for that matter, if you have already made contact and they are expecting your information, otherwise stick to old-fashioned delivery methods.

Develop a system to stay organized about where and when you applied for positions. You could ruin your chances with an employer if you mistakenly refer to them by a competitor's name over the phone or contact them more than once in the same time period.

Your attitude comes through in your letters and on the telephone. Be extremely courteous and for goodness sake, do not get pushy! Speaking from experience with obnoxious applicants, no one owes you an opportunity.

Exhaust every resource when pursuing internships and apply for more than one. Contact as many prospects and set up as many interviews as possible. Be prepared to give a 15 second promotion regarding your skills, strengths and reason you want to work for them. Many internships are acquired using this technique.

Interview Tips

To this point in the book we have covered how to find an internship, which may seem to be the easy part to those who dread "the interview". You may be the best-qualified candidate for the job but be one who struggles through an interview and does not get selected.

If you have received a call inviting you to interview, take heart! It means they believe you may be the one to hire but they want to know for sure. The interview gives both you and a potential employer a chance to evaluate each other.

In the survey, those who hire were asked what tips they would give design students regarding the job interview. The quotes listed below were their answers:

- "Be yourself and show the most positive parts of you, your work and personality."

- "Dress appropriately."

- "Be cheerful, business like, optimistic, self-assured, relaxed and focused."

- "Know the company you are interviewing with. Have something in common to talk to them about."

- "Bring examples of the drawings you have produced, along with examples of your design work."

- "Be honest and forthright, be open in discussing what you want, be prompt for interview, be prepared for unusual questions, be willing to share yourself in an authentic way."

- "Come early. Research the firm you are interviewing and bring actual work."

- "Don't wear revealing clothing or look like you just got up. Have a resume and a portfolio, not just a disk. Some of us are old and can't see details on a disk. Be on time."

- "Be prompt, well groomed, know the company having visited the website, know what we do, be prepared to sell the work in your portfolio, good energy, composure, ask good questions."

- "Act positive but know that you are still learning. Do not oversell your abilities."

- "Dress professionally, be on time, and smile."

- "Be on time, or better yet, about 4 minutes early. Allow for traffic, parking, etc. Dress for the job. This does not mean school clothes. Go out and get an outfit for interviews, neat from shoes up. Be enthusiastic."

- "Be yourself. Don't apologize for anything, be on time, be organized."

- "Arrive early, dress professionally, don't talk too much about yourself where the interviewer only gets to ask you one question before the time is up. Answer questions asked."

- "Focus less on the portfolio and how beautiful your student projects were. Emphasize organizational skills, any previous office experience, and other skills such as computer skills. Many interns have nice looking portfolios....the other skills make the difference."

- "Respect the interviewers time. Be prepared for short interviews at the spur of the moment. Be yourself as much as possible."

- "Dress appropriately. Shower and have clean hair. Do not wear perfume. Be prepared to show portfolio in a short period of time. Don't elaborate. Bring example of printing skills. Bring a written bio on your skill levels of office and computer work and any work experience you have previously had, bring written recommendation from your former employer."

- "Be positive. Do not recite every "fair employment" rule nor ask how often there is a review or paid vacation, etc. Employers know that stuff and are looking for people with a passion for design work. Show your boards & drawings only….not associates."

- "Be on time, if not 5-10 minutes early. Be calm and focused, smile, be prepared and bring a great portfolio and résumé with you."

- "Be neatly dressed, not over dressed. Be prepared to express your personal career goals and what you would like to achieve in their prospective job."

- "Walk in confidently and not be intimidated to ask questions. Promote good qualities and think about what would set you apart from other candidates."

- "Don't expect too much."

- "Be polite, attentive, inquisitive and well dressed – professionally."

- "Be yourself. Research the company you are interviewing with. Dress appropriately. Be specific on what you want to get out of the internship."

- "Have prepared questions for the firm, think through possible answers to firm's questions prior to the interview, and relax."

- "Come prepared. Research the firm before the interview. Have multiple copies of your resume. Bring portfolio and be ready to give a rehearsed presentation. We understand most of your portfolio is schoolwork - all the more reason you should be able to put on a show. Don't be a "know it all". Don't talk too much – or too little."

- "Check the condition of your portfolio for signs of wear and tear. Show only your best work."

From the number of times mentioned by many different designers, do you get the impression being on time, dressing appropriately and being yourself are important? Take note of tips mentioned multiple times and make sure you follow them when you interview.

At the end of the interview, before you leave, be sure to ask when the employer expects to make the hiring decision and find out about their follow-up procedures. If possible, get a business card from each person involved in the interview so you will have his or her correct name, title and address.

After the Interview Follow-up

Be proactive and consider follow-up as part of your job search process. Proper follow-up can give you the edge in getting the job over others who interviewed for the position by showing you have a high level of professionalism.

After the interview, there are two follow-up strategies you need to complete: what to do during the first few days following the interview and how to follow-up after receiving an offer.

Following the interview -

- Within two business days, send a letter to the interviewer expressing your appreciation for the employer's interest in you. Reiterate your interest in their organization and give a brief review of your qualifications. This will keep you in the forefront of their mind as well as demonstrate you have good manners and know how to write a thank-you letter.

- Send individual thank you notes to each person who interviewed you. They can essentially be worded the same but should vary a bit to make each one more personal, especially in case they compare notes.

- Be sure to send thank you notes after *each* interview and never, ever have any misspellings or typos!

- Alert your references that they may be getting a phone call from the potential employer.

- Follow up with any information the employer may have asked you to provide.

- Continue to job hunt and interview for other positions, even if you feel confident that you will get the job offer. Don't sit back and wait.

- If more than a week has passed beyond the date you were told you would hear from the employer, call or email to politely inquire about the decision status. Continue to show your enthusiasm and desire for the position without making it seem as though you are desperate.

After receiving an offer –

- If you receive an offer before you have finished all your interviews, find out when they need a decision and consider asking for an extension if you still have other interviews scheduled.

- It is acceptable to say yes to offers over the phone but also ask for the offer in writing. The written offer will usually include necessary details associated with the position including start date, salary and location.

- When you receive an offer, always accept in writing and reiterate terms discussed to ensure you and your new employer are in agreement.

- If you receive multiple offers, weigh each one carefully considering location, size and type of company. Determine which one will best help you to reach your goals.

- If you decline an offer, do so promptly with courtesy and respect. Exhibit a high level of professionalism. You may have contact with them at some point in the future.

- Always, always, follow-up with a thank you note.

Create an Internship That Does Not Exist

If the company you would like to intern with already has an existing internship program, you need only prepare and apply for the position. However, if they do not have a program set up, you many need to create one.

Research the company in-depth and determine why they might need the assistance of an intern. You know "what's in it for you", but what's in it for them?

Find out whom you should contact. The ideal person would be the one who has the authority to make the final decision. However, managers sometimes have a need but do not seek approval for new personnel until they have found a qualified candidate.

Send your resume with a strong letter of application showing why you want to work for them, making sure to note the benefits the company would receive. Many companies will be more willing to help you if they can see the value you would bring to their business.

Follow-up with a telephone call and try to set up an interview. Be genuine and sincere, as positions are sometimes created to accommodate a terrific person who proactively contacts a business. Also, the personal contact greatly enhances your chances as compared to an anonymous letter.

Ask about part-time positions and summer jobs they may offer. Do they need assistance maintaining the resource library and scheduling vendor updates? The addition of a structured program to these jobs could create the equivalent of an internship.

It will take research and resourcefulness but you may find it is well worth your time, as you will be practicing the job-hunting skills you will need later when you seek a full-time position.

Top Tips (on Getting an Internship) From Those Who Hire

You have just learned how to find and get an internship, but have you ever wondered what those who hire have to say about the process? What specific qualities do they look for in an applicant?

We asked those who make the hiring decision what "top tips" they would give interns regarding how to get an internship and what an employer looks for in a job candidate.

The following are direct quotes from the surveys they completed:

- "Good CAD skills."

- "Know the job, the employer before the interview and the type of work the designer does."

- "Know a lot about the firm you want to work with and especially the person who is going to interview you."

- "Go to events in the design community. It is fairly small and people will recognize you. ASID events are educational and current."

- "Persistence."

- "Come with a good portfolio presentation and an attitude of eagerness to learn anything and everything about the profession."

- "Show what you can do to help the company. Look and act sharp, like you really want to be a successful designer."

45

- "Be fairly aggressive in your search for the right firm. Tailor your portfolio to the kind of work the firm does. Sell your strengths."

- "Emphasize all of your skills. Portfolios are important, but are only PART of the complete package."

- "Research the company you want to work for – impress the employer with how much you know about them and want to be integrated into the regular cycle of work/projects in house."

- "Have a recommendation from another designer."

- "Keep trying. My best intern ever was a C-average Home Ec Graduate – levelheaded problem solver, quick study."

- "Offer a diverse mix of learning experiences."

- "Talent and personality."

- "Submit resume, answer all questions asked before in a timely and professional manner. Show up for interview prepared and on time & be flexible in terms of what you can provide."

- "Approach it like a real interview and be prepared. Do research on the company; be realistic about what you will be working on."

- "An interested, no nonsense applicant who loves interior design and wants to show what they can do at this point in their career."

- "Someone who is definitely a self-starter and doesn't have to be told each and every thing to do. Organized. Someone who represents the company well."

- "Self motivated, personality, dress attire."

- "Technical skills: AutoCAD, REVIT, general computer skills: Word, excel, etc; Good attitude, appropriate dress, team player."

- "Potential professionalism."

- "Self-starters, energetic, open people who want to work in a collaborative environment. Will go the extra distance and have a strong work ethic, able to meet the many challenges that occur regularly in this business."

- "Adequate skill level, professionalism, great attitude."

- "Good attitude, desire to work and contribute. We don't expect professional quality work, but imagination, CAD and other computer skills."

- "Design talent willingness to help in any task needed."

- "Poise and confidence, portfolio presentation, other skills and activities of interest."

- "Professionalism, good manners, flexibility."

- "Experience (even office experience), punctuality, reliability, enthusiasm."

- "Be persistent, ask for internship, be available, be on time

- "Full range of skills, not just a nice portfolio."

- "Self-starter attitude. Someone interested in turning the internship into a longer relationship (due to the investment the employer is making)."

- "Be prepared. Know the company you are interviewing with, know what you want out of the internship, have your portfolio and resume in good order, dress appropriately."

- "Familiarity with fabrics, furniture, designer software programs like Studio IT, nice CAD dwgs."

- "Eager to learn not just to get ahead, willingness to work hard, positive can do attitude."

- "Keen desire to work hard and learn. A design sensibility that matches ours (do your research). A positive, upbeat or easy-going personality that will work as a team with other staff members."

- "Most of the time, employers are looking for someone to just "fill" in. Employers get many job applications, so sometimes choosing one person is random. However, once that person is selected, they expect that position to float and fill in whenever and wherever necessary. I am always looking for someone who is trainable, so flexibility is the key. Follow up on the interview, and let them know that you are readily available."

Hopefully, given in this chapter are key words of advice which if followed will lead you to success in getting the internship you want. Take some time now to answer the questions at the beginning of the chapter if you have not done so already. Do your self-assessment and see how you rate against the tips from professionals that are listed above. Put a plan into action on how to improve your skills and abilities, then go get your job!

Chapter 4:
Internship Tips for Success

So far you have learned why you need to intern and how to find and get an internship. You have followed the advice given and have landed the internship you wanted! Right? So now what?

If you are receiving credit, your internship will have to be approved by your school. Your academic advisor or sponsor will need to agree to supervise and evaluate your experience. Set up a regular meeting schedule to keep them abreast of your difficulties as well as your accomplishments. Be a good listener and learn as much as you can during these meetings.

Next, get ready to work! Reread your goals and get your mind set for success. The tips given in this chapter will help you know what to expect and how to best maximize your experience tuning you in to what you should and should not do as an intern.

Expectations of an Intern vs. Reality of the Job

Most of your time spent in school entails learning the principles and elements of design and how to apply them. This involves the design of space as well as how to use materials and components to build, furnish and accent your design. You learn how to create an environment that takes into consideration the health, safety and welfare of the occupants.

Some of your class time is spent discussing the business of design. This may include proposals and contracts, marketing and running a business, processes of a project from beginning to end and dealing with clients, consultants and suppliers. All of these are the heart of an interior design job.

As an interior design intern, what you expect to be doing and the realities of the job can be vastly different. You might be expecting to actually get to design an interior space, which will most likely not be the case. If you are not informed and prepared, your internship may be an unpleasant and unrewarding experience.

You should have a clear idea of what is expected of you and what you should expect from an employer before you start. You do not want to be disappointed and no one likes an intern with unrealistic expectations or delusions of grandeur.

This is a Job, Not a Class

First and foremost, work and college are different so, you will need to adjust. Faculty may not penalize you if you fly into class five minutes late or if you miss a class or two. You are paying to go to college so it is your loss, not theirs.

An employer, however, is paying you to work so tardiness and absenteeism are not acceptable. You do not have the option of sleeping in or missing a day if you stayed up too late the night before. Being late or missing work is a signal of disrespect for other's time and a lack of interest in the job.

Designers work on projects with deadlines, almost on a daily basis. When an intern is hired, they are included in the project schedule and given tasks to complete. Being late and missing work can cause others to have heavier workloads, or worse, deadlines to be missed.

Promptness signals eagerness, responsibility and respect for others. Being on time might seem obvious, but it is important in making a good impression so at least be on time, but better yet, be early. You also do not have the luxury of taking extra long lunch breaks so don't get lazy.

Stay focused on the present and remember where you are. Stay out of the past *and* the future. Co-workers do not want every word you speak to be about 'how we do this at school' or what your dream job will be when you graduate.

Also know at work you will not receive as much feedback regarding your performance or be asked to share your opinion as often as you do in school. You may not be asked to solve any major problems either. Use your internship as a time to observe and learn.

What Will They Expect of You?

The best way to find out what an employer expects of you is to ask. Sit down with your supervisor and discuss the details and logistics of your position. Agree on a detailed job description and performance expectations so you have a clear idea of what is expected of you when you start.

The quality of your work should be 'A' level. You should produce high quality, careful work for your level of expertise, but don't forget you are a beginner. Give attention to the little details such as making sure holes punched in documents are all aligned, pages copied are straight and materials are filed in proper order. The little things you do make a big difference in how your work is viewed.

Most assignments you will be given will have a deadline. *Always* ask when you need to have the task completed and never assume you can finish it 'tomorrow'. Projects are comprised of many small parts and delay in completing your assignment could hold up everyone else. Make it a priority to finish it on time, or earlier if possible. Be prompt while at the same time maintaining high quality work.

Strive for excellence, not perfection. Check and double-check your work for accuracy and be sure all names are spelled correctly. Use spell check on documents and make sure text is correct on presentations and plans. When creating presentation boards, be sure edges are clean cut and materials mounted are straight. You want to be known for the quality of your work.

Communication involves both written and oral skills. By now you have learned to read, write and possibly speak well, but how well do you listen? Being a good listener is essential for interior designers. If you cannot listen to and follow directions of superiors, how can you expect to listen to and follow clients' wishes? Learn to listen to directions given, be attentive, alert and take notes on what is being said so you will have fewer mistakes.

Learn to provide excellent customer service when dealing with clients and others. Always be helpful and courteous. They are not interruptions to your work and you are not doing them a favor by serving. Clients are the purpose of your work and are doing you a favor by giving you a chance to serve. Your employer will expect you to represent them well.

Be self-sufficient and learn to get the answers yourself when possible. Understand that some general office work is part of the job. All internships, and most jobs for that matter, involve some menial tasks such as filing, faxing and photocopying. Expect some busywork and show you can do it efficiently.

Remember, your mother does not work there so be sure to clean up after yourself. That includes your dishes, utensils and place at the table in the break room after you eat lunch. Keep your workspace clean and well organized. When you see something that needs done, do it. Do not wait to be told what to do. (Does that sound like something your parents have told you?)

The resource library is a prime example of a never-ending task. Because of the nature of design, there is always some material or catalog that needs re-filed or updated. This is a great way to become familiar with resources and gain valuable knowledge about manufacturer's specification methods.

Never, ever do personal shopping, send personal email or send instant messages when you are on the clock. Conduct yourself with the highest of professional ethics. Office supplies are not for personal use, so do the right thing. Remember you are there to help build a business by giving of yourself, not continually taking from others.

What to do When You Start

The first day on any job can evoke a multitude of emotions ranging from anxiety to excitement. First impressions are important. This includes your impression of the company as well as their impression of you. What you do your first week can set the tone for the duration of your internship.

There are several things you should do when you start that will make your job less stressful and help you make a great lasting impression.

Following your arrival the first day, most likely the first item of business will be a brief introduction to co-workers. Try to remember as many names as possible, what their particular job responsibility is and where their office is located.

Besides your direct supervisor, there is usually one person who knows where to find anything you need. Take notice of whom this person is and where to find them.

Smile, be friendly (but not too chatty) and introduce yourself to everyone. Don't be afraid to go up to a co-worker and introduce yourself if you missed them during initial introductions. The more people you know the better.

Next, get acquainted with your surroundings. Get a feel for the office layout and where to find office equipment such as plotters, copiers and the fax machine. Locate the resource library, file cabinets, workroom and conference rooms. Also, make sure you know where to find the basics such as supply storage, break area and restrooms. Knowing your way around quickly will make your job much easier.

Inspect your assigned workspace and get familiar with operation of the telephone and computer. Make sure you have the supplies and equipment you need so you can be prepared for your first assignment.

Start the first day to demonstrate exceptional work ethic. Without being too aggressive or bossy, show you are a 'can do' type person. Be a second miler and go beyond the call of duty, but without being a 'kiss-up'. Just be helpful and have a great attitude.

If you have not already done so, begin learning as much as you can about the organization. As you work, find out a little about the history of the company and their goals. Who are their clients and their consultants as well as competitors? What type and size of projects do they have?

Observe the company culture. Do people work together in teams or separately? Is there a lot of friendly banter or mostly gossiping? Do employees look like they love their job or look stressed? The work atmosphere can give clues about the industry as a whole and whether this company is right for you or not.

As you are given tasks to do, try not to worry if your work is not perfect. They know you are there to learn and will make mistakes in the beginning. Ask questions if you do not understand something and admit when you do not know the answer. You are a student and they know that. Gradually ask for more responsibility and always look for things to do. Show initiative!

Introduce new ideas and procedures gradually. Remember you are there to learn so avoid trying to change too much too soon. Advice is best taken when asked for, so offer ideas only when asked.

Maximize the Experience

Getting as much out of your internship as possible will take focused effort on your part. Use the fact that you are a student to your advantage. Because you are a student, you are not threatening and often have access to meetings and areas of the company other employees do not.

Everyone wants to help a student learn (well, almost everyone). Do not be afraid to talk with people and do not be intimidated because you are a student. Realize co-workers may be too busy to roll out the red carpet so you may have to make the first move.

Keeping a journal of your activities may be required by your school in order for you to receive credit for your internship. You should maintain it on a daily or at least a weekly basis but be sure you do this on your own time and keep it at home. You do not want co-workers accidentally accessing your private thoughts and observations. A journal is also a great place to record names and information about contacts you make.

If keeping a journal is not required, keep one anyway. It will be helpful in assessing your experience by providing a record of your growth and development over the course of the internship. It will also help you articulate during an interview when asked about your experience and be useful when updating your resume'.

Focus on Learning

Be a sponge! Soak up every bit of knowledge you can. Read everything you can get your hands on including proposals, contracts, meeting minutes, memos, and correspondence. Review plans, shop drawings, submittals and specifications. Keep informed about industry news and products through trade magazines. Read to get a good understanding of how each of these is used in the business.

Get in the information loop. Not all decisions are made in the conference room and training manuals do not have all the answers. Listen to and learn from what is being said when working on projects. Talk with people in different departments as well as clients and vendors.

Attend as many meetings and conferences as you can. Pay attention to how people talk to one another and discuss issues. You can learn a lot from watching and listening to others.

Everything has a purpose, so learn how the small tasks fit into the big picture. Do not gripe about the small stuff either as there is always something to learn by doing it. If you feel like you are not learning enough or being challenged enough, ask for more responsibility.

Be open-minded about new ideas and procedures. Remember that you are just beginning to learn the business and your teachers have not you taught everything. Try to not be defensive and accept constructive criticism graciously as it will help you grow.

Participate in extra-curricular activities such as field trips, continuing education seminars, and luncheons whenever possible. These may be some of your best learning experiences and most memorable of your internship.

Learn the Art of Networking

So just what is networking? It is the process of making contact and exchanging information with other people while building relationships. This personal set of contacts may be able to help you in some way and you may be able to help them too.

When you are networking, you are not just being friendly, 'schmoozing' or giving a personal sales pitch. You are attentively and consciously meeting people, remembering who they are and what they do and beginning to exchange information with them over time.

Developing a network is a lifelong process. The professional relationships you cultivate with people both inside and outside the industry will create more opportunities for yourself for years to come. Networking will often result in a job prospect that did not exist before you networked!

So whom do you network with? Everybody! Specifically network with those you meet at the job site such as co-workers, manufacturer's reps and vendors. You should also get to know other designers, architects and consultants you meet at seminars, conferences and events. These are all in addition to your family, friends and professors from school.

Be sure to include networking with people you meet in other industries as they can lead you to job and project opportunities. You never know when someone at the nearby sandwich shop or bank will give you the lead of a lifetime.

A few words of warning about social networking sites on the Internet – be careful what you share. Companies do search the Internet for information about potential employees. Remember the old adage, "anything you say can be repeated". Anything you post online can be copied and pasted to reemerge without warning or permission.

Professional networking sites are great places to search for jobs, post your resume and increase your visibility. Connect with groups of interest within the industry and ask questions to gain information or assistance, however, make sure the questions are genuine as phonies are easily spotted and subsequently ignored.

No matter who you contact or how, it is important to remember the following etiquette when networking:

- Be gracious with those who give of their time and do not overstay your welcome, nor "return to the well" too many times.
- Send thank you notes when people take time to meet with you.
- Always be professional, courteous and considerate.
- Be genuine and possess a sincere desire to learn.
- Be interested in people you meet as most people enjoy the chance to tell you about their careers and activities.
- Be honest and use good judgment when asking for advice.
- Give back – know enough about the people you meet to keep their needs in mind so you can pass along contacts and ideas that will interest them.
- Stay in touch and update people in your network when you make changes in your progress or job status.

Networking can be used in many ways in a job search or throughout your career to conduct project research, obtain career advice or obtain information about organizations for which you might want to work. It is an art that when developed properly can result in helpful information and job possibilities.

People Who Can Help You

During your internship, you will have the opportunity to meet many people who can be powerful sources of information and assistance in your interior design training. Some will be inside the organization and some outside.

Inside the Organization

- Interns - If there are any fellow interns, be sure to meet and share ideas, even if they are not in your particular department. They can be a good support system and be loaded with information about the company.

- Department colleagues – These will most likely be the ones you work most closely with, however they are probably going to be the busiest. They will be your main source of growth and learning, so take the lead in getting to know them. You may be assigned to assist them with projects. Ask intelligent questions and show your willingness to help, even with the small stuff. Once they see you can be trusted, you will probably be asked to do more.

- Direct Supervisor – They might be too busy to work much with you so you may need to take the lead to build a good relationship. They also may not have the best mentoring skills. Check in periodically to update them on what you have been learning and review your goals. Show genuine interest in the work and let them know you are willing to take on additional tasks.

- Administrative Staff – Without support staff, the organization would not run. They are the nuts and bolts of the company, so get to know them and show them respect. They can be a great source of information to help you accomplish your goals and learn the 'unspoken' rules of the company.

•Others Within the Company – At sometime during your internship, you should touch base with those that you do not work with directly. Find out what they do for the company and get advice or suggestions regarding career path. Be careful that you are not perceived as wasting time or going beyond your boundaries by wandering around introducing yourself to people in other departments. Never take on extra work from someone in another department without permission from your supervisor.

Outside the Organization

- Manufacturer's Reps – An invaluable source of knowledge about much more than just their product line, they have a large network of designers and organizations that they frequently contact. Reps often know of job openings before they are advertised. From their years in the business, they can be walking encyclopedias on their particular segment of the industry.

- Furniture Dealers – They also have a large network of contacts, designers as well as businesses, and can be a great source for jobs in the industry as well as those that are industry related. Dealers can help you understand the procurement process and associated problems. They can also help you with sourcing products that help you reach your design objective.

- Consultants – These can be great sources of technical information. Be sure to tap into the specialized knowledge consultants have to help you understand your limitations as well as possibilities in design.

- Designers – During local events, you may have a chance to network with other designers, and architects for that matter. Those at other organizations will be doing similar projects but may use different methods. Short question and answer meetings with them may give you an idea about the various processes used to reach a design solution.

Learn as much as you can from the people who are the superstar performers and most respected in the company. "Hitch your wagon to a star" as they say, but do so without trying to make them your personal tutor.

Also, you never know when you will see someone later in your career so do not burn any bridges. You need as many people on your side as possible helping you apply what you have learned.

Internship Etiquette

Business etiquette is presenting yourself by displaying good manners, common courtesy and respect for others while being comfortable around them and making them feel comfortable around you. This is a must in the work field and should become habitual for you if you want to be successful.

Internship etiquette includes business etiquette, but goes one step further to include acceptable behavior and manners *at your internship site*. The problem is the rules are seldom spelled out and are not the same for any two organizations. You will need to do some quick observation to determine what is acceptable and what is not. This is kind of like being a freshman again. Watch the 'seniors' and follow what they are doing.

Basic Social Skills

There are plenty of books available on etiquette that you can use to help you evaluate your basic social skills. Knowing the basics will set you apart as a professional and cause superiors notice you, so take time to learn the following:

Proper Introductions

- Always greet people you meet with a smile – your first impression should be a positive one.

- Take the initiative to volunteer your own name first and speak clearly. Always use first and last name, do not use first name only in introductions.

- Always extend your hand, looking the person in the eyes when you speak.

- Use a firm, brief handshake while making eye contact.

- Be sure to include everyone in the group and avoid the worst mistake - no introduction at all!

General Conversation

- Limit the use of the word 'I'.

- Focus on the other person rather than yourself.

- Include all people present.

- Watch your language and lose the lingo. Using expressions used on campus such as 'hey, cool' will tell people you are not yet professional material.

- Listen to the language of those around you and take clues from them on how you should speak.

- When you receive a compliment for any reason, simply smile say 'thank you'. You do not need to reply with an explanation or reciprocal compliment.

Telephone Communication

- Always answer the telephone pleasantly, immediately giving your own name to the caller.

- When making a call, give your own name before you state your business. This underscores that a person of value is making the call.

- Speak clearly with enthusiasm.

- Return calls promptly.

- When leaving voice mail messages, leave your name and call back number. Speak the number slowly and repeat it twice. This makes it easier for the one you called to jot down your number without having to replay the message.

- Turn your cell phones off in meetings and remember, others can hear your conversation.

General Basics

- Do not sit down in someone's office until invited to do so.

- Watch your posture - stand tall and sit up straight

- Keep your feet off the furniture.

- Hats off inside.

- Do not chew gum.

- Do not reach across someone for something at a table or desk.

If you want to make points in the world of work, learn how to handle hellos, good-byes and the basic courtesies of speech and action. These can win friends or turn people off, so practice before you start your internship!

Professional Behavior

One of the quickest ways to kill an internship is by being negative. No one likes to be around someone who is constantly whining or complaining. The energy used complaining could be spent getting work completed!

Be careful what you say and *never* make negative comments about people or assignments. You can talk about issues, projects and the work environment (with caution), but refrain from talking about people. You would be surprised how quickly your comments get back to your employer.

Keeping confidential information confidential is essential. Whatever someone tells you should remain with you. Do not repeat everything you hear. Steer clear of interoffice politics and avoid taking sides. Not all discussions will include you so do not be hurt if you are left out. Some issues are for staff only.

Watch your nonverbal communication or body language. Do you frown when you think? It could be misread as anger instead of deep in thought. Do you constantly fix your hair? It could be misread as unprepared instead of bad haircut. Do you always fold your arms when you talk to others? Warming your cold hands could be mistaken as boredom. Be aware of the signals you are sending. An accurate 'first' reading of body language is necessary because there may not be a second chance.

Conduct yourself with integrity. If you are a person of integrity, you will work just as hard when supervisors are present as when they are not. Be responsible for your actions. When you say you will do something, do it. When you make a mistake, take responsibility for it. Making excuses and pointing fingers will not get you ahead.

Follow the chain of command and know the formal as well as informal reporting structure. Know the unspoken rule: Do not go around, behind or over anyone. Be sensitive to the needs of others and not just interested in your own career path.

It is *extremely* important that you be on time. This applies to any drawings or project tasks that are due as well as arriving at the workplace. Budget extra time for getting the work done as it usually takes longer to complete a task than we expect.

It is best to budget extra time when traveling but sometimes the unexpected arises. It is important to call immediately and speak directly with your supervisor if you encounter a problem that causes you to be late. Also, call if you have a serious illness or family emergency that justifies an absence.

Be a good ambassador and ever mindful that you reflect your school. How you perform and behave could affect the future of other interns from your school.

Dress for Respect, Groom for Confidence

One of the biggest complaints given about interns is the lack of professional dress. What is commonplace on campus is usually not acceptable in the workplace. So, how do you rate here? Do you have any clothing suitable for work in a design office?

It would be a good idea to take an in-depth inventory of the clothing in your closet. Begin during college to transition your wardrobe from the school casual/slouch look to professional attire. Then you will have suitable clothing when you begin your internship and be prepared for when you graduate and start to work.

Dressing appropriately is very important. If you do not know what this is, during your interviews or research, look around you at what others are wearing. What kind of accessories are the norms? What are the hairstyles? Get a book on dressing for success and learn the basics. Also, avoid wearing perfume, cologne or scented hairspray but do wear deodorant!

It is ok to call the receptionist and ask about the dress code if this was not made clear when you accepted the position. Once you have started work, model your dress after your supervisor and other professional staff and you cannot go wrong.

If you want respect, dress for it. Wear clothing that flatters you but does not reveal everything! Dress for a specific image and that means 'designer' not model or rock star. Take some advice from those who hire.

It would be best to avoid extreme hairstyles, extra piercings and visible tattoos as they are a "turn-off" to employers and you come across as unprofessional.

What about your physical appearance? Are you neat and clean? Do you have good hygiene and grooming standards? Or do you always look like you just rolled out of bed? What does your posture say about you – enthusiastic or slacker?

Believe it or not, good grooming will increase your feelings of self-worth enabling your confidence to grow. The less you have to worry about how you look, the better. You will then be more able to concentrate on doing a good job. You want your employer and co-workers to notice your work, not your dress and grooming.

When you walk in the door of your internship site, you are no longer a student. You will be judged on how you look first, speak next and abilities last. First impressions have a lasting effect and your appearance can be a big factor in making or breaking your internship.

Meals with Co-workers and Clients

Business meals provide an opportunity to interact socially while doing business. As an intern you may be invited to attend a business meal with other project team members or your supervisor. It is unlikely you will be asked to attend a meal alone with a client. You may also be the one inviting others to meet with you to seek professional advice or network with them.

The traditional business meal is lunch however, breakfast or dinner are options depending on which best fits the purpose. One hour is not sufficient for a meeting so be prepared to allocate one to two hours in order to get anything accomplished. Business dinners may last anywhere from 2-4 hours.

The first consideration is whom it is productive for you to have a business meal with and where it should be held. If you set up the meeting, it is appropriate for you to pick up the tab. Where the meal meeting is held should be determined by your business needs and reflect the level of the person you are meeting. You should have a list of three places from which to choose and ask your guest where they would like to meet.

Invite them early, not at the last minute. Be sure to tell your guest the nature of the business you would like to discuss so they can bring any appropriate materials. Reconfirm the time and place the day before

If possible, reserve a table in advance so you start your meeting on time. Stick to business during the meeting. It is easy to get distracted in a pleasant environment.

Show the same consideration for coworkers as you do for clients if the meal is for business. For purely social interaction, you may be a little more relaxed but remember to keep within your allotted lunchtime.

You may have the opportunity to attend luncheons provided by manufacturer's reps or vendors where they present their product line. In return for the designers giving up lunchtime to listen to a presentation, the reps provide lunch for all attending. These will be attended by co-workers and may be in-house or at a different location depending on the size of your company.

Lunch n' Learns, as they are sometimes called, can be a great resource for you, not only for the product information but the networking contact. They are usually set up weeks in advance. Be thoughtful of those offering to bring in lunch in exchange for your time and be there if you said you would attend. If a conflict in your schedule arises, be courteous and let the rep know you will not be attending.

(For more information about business meal etiquette, see Appendix B at the end of the book.)

Tips From Designers

During your internship, you will most likely be working directly with other designers. They can be great mentors during your journey by helping you learn or be stumbling blocks in your path by brushing you off and not utilizing your time.

The quotes below were replies given in the study regarding things to do and to absolutely *not* do as an intern. If you want to have a successful internship, follow these tips from designers as they voiced their opinions and gave advice to future interns.

Designers' "Pet Peeves" Regarding Interns

- "No desire to learn and be a real part of the design work that goes on here. Continually picturing themselves as temporary help."

- "Unmotivated people, having to be told what to do, no initiative."

- "First impressions count a lot – don't show up and act as if you are a still teenager. Professional attire is important, you are not auditioning for a rock band."

- "Aren't always willing to do what it takes to get the job done. Oblivious to deadlines."

- "Not understanding the full range of skills and activities that make up being a designer, the non-design components of the profession."

- "They use more than they give."

- "Not enough related or office work experience."

- "You are there to work. The head designer is not there to be your unpaid private tutor. Keep eyes open and mouth shut."

- "Dress code is ignored. Asking so many questions that there is no time to work. Making so many assumptions that nothing is done correctly."

- "Slow work, attitude, not showing up on time or missing days of work."

- "Having your cell phone on and wasting time talking to friends, text messaging, clock watching, being late."

- "Do not act as is you know it all. You are there to learn and experience what it is like to work in an office atmosphere which is very different from an educational atmosphere."

- "Assume you will be designing at all times. Treating the internship as a temporary break time job."

- "Never criticize the designers in front of other staff or clients. Do not bring your child to work. Do not take the first ½ hour combing hair & sharpening pencils. Don't leave before closing time."

- "Don't let pressure of deadlines get to you. Don't assume anything, get confirmation. Don't ask TOO many questions, answers will come."

- "Chat too much, be a know-it-all, sit and wait for more work, waste time."

- "Be late, socialize too much."

You want to avoid doing or being like the interns mentioned in the negative comments listed above. Again, take each comment and determine what the opposite positive action would be. Make sure you do those things and add to it the tips listed below.

Top Tips from Designers of Thing to be Sure to Do

- "Always stay busy, wanting to find other things to do around the offices or wherever we may be. Always be productive. Picture yourself actually working permanently at this job."

- "Network, get to know every department of the company."

- "Do what you are asked to do in a professional manner, listen and ask questions, be personable and show interest in what you are doing. Show creativity and initiative in tasks."

- "Be on time, complete work in a timely fashion. Check your work before handing it over, ask questions if you are not sure."

- "Be on time, be enthusiastic, be polite, be organized."

- "Ask questions when you do not understand what is expected, have an interest in all aspects of the profession."

- "Be aware of all office communications. Take orders gracefully. Be willing to go into overtime mode. Offer to help others regardless of skill level. When overwhelmed, ask direct boss how to prioritize."

- "Ask for more work when you have completed tasks. Be on time, stay longer than requested."

Take all the tips that have been given and begin to apply them. By keeping your expectations and reality aligned, maximizing the experience by learning everything you can and maintaining a professional appearance, you will have a successful internship.

Chapter 5:
How to Get Them to Keep You

You got the internship you wanted, you like the people, the job and the company. Now, how do you get them to keep you on payroll full-time after the internship is completed? How do you get them to offer you a job?

Every employer wants to hire only the best and brightest. They want someone who will be an asset to their company, not a liability. They want an employee that will make their workload easier, not more difficult. They want someone who can be trusted to work hard and will do a great job.

The goal of eventually landing a permanent position with the company should have been set before you began your internship and should be reflected in your behavior.

To reach your goal, there are a couple of specific things to do that will make you valuable and land you a job. Sometimes, doing these will even open doors that are closed or cause a position to be created just for you.

Check Your Attitude

The number one tip you need to know is just how much difference your attitude makes in getting them to keep you. You need to make sure you have a positive, can-do attitude because a bad one is without a doubt your ticket out the door!

An employer should feel comfortable asking you to handle any task without receiving any attitude in return. If it is important enough for them to ask you to do it, there must be a reason, even if you think it is a meaningless task. Do not assume your education places you above low-level tasks. Have an "I'll do whatever it takes" and eager-to-learn attitude.

One of my favorite analogies about attitude comes from Bob Proctor, author, lecturer and coach in the self-motivation arena. He said we often sit in front an empty fireplace saying, "Give me some heat". What we fail to realize is that we have to put the wood in first before we can get any heat.

You may be studying design and think you are ready to begin designing actual projects. However, prior to receiving that opportunity, you have to prove some things about your work ethic and abilities. You have to prove you can be trusted before an employer will let you design projects that are the lifeblood of a company. Also, if you want them to keep you, you must first put some "wood in the fireplace".

Realize an employer watches every move you make and building their trust begins with menial tasks like photocopying. If you can't be trusted to handle the small stuff, how can they trust you with the big stuff? It is just common sense. Do the best you can on any task, no matter how small.

Show your willingness to go beyond what is in the job description for your internship. Seek out extra work and look for ways to make your employer's and co-workers' jobs easier. You will make a good impression if do.

You may be a star student but do not assume you know everything. If you did, you would not need to intern! Ask enough questions to show your desire to learn but not enough to be annoying. Remember to show initiative. They want you to learn without having to constantly hold your hand.

Most of the time, design is a collaborative effort. Showing you can work well with a team will be important. Remember what you learned in kindergarten – "play well with others" and show you can fit in.

Find a Niche, Fill a Need

You can become invaluable to your employer by filling a need. Look around at the company and observe which tasks have to be outsourced or are not completed with efficiency. Are these skills you already have or can develop?

Often, business owners who have been around a while (ok, the old guys!) are not technologically savvy. They rely on others for IT and computer skills. Being a computer expert will often put your name on the "keeper" list quicker than anything else.

Having knowledge of and being able to use software such as Photoshop, Illustrator, and Power Point will give you a great advantage. Knowing AutoCAD is a must for most firms and the higher your skill level the better.

Familiarity with hardware such as printers, plotters and media storage is an added bonus too. Spend time before your internship increasing your knowledge base in these areas so you can impress your employer with your abilities at the start of your internship.

Saving your employer time and money will give you the edge in getting hired full-time. The wider your range of skills, the more valuable you will be.

Ask for the Job!

Some employers may not realize you are interested in getting the job unless you ask, so do not be shy in asking about a permanent position. Keep track of your accomplishments and contributions (one of the reasons why you keep a journal) so you can present this list when you make your pitch to remain as a full-time employee after your internship.

At the end of your internship, you may still have courses to complete and are not yet ready to work full-time. If so, leave on the best possible terms. Keep in contact with your supervisor and others within the company who make the hiring decision. If you have made a great impression, chances are they will ask you to return after you graduate.

What an Employer Does NOT Want

If you want to know why employers do not ask interns to return, read on. From experiences in the past, they have had the same recurring problems too many times. I have tried to cover all these issues in this book hoping to help you avoid being one of the problem interns.

Here are quotes from designers on why they do not ask an intern to return. Take note!

- "Some students are only doing an internship to satisfy their college graduation requirements and it is really obvious after two weeks of working with them."

- "Making personal phone calls and not listening to what is wanted and needed."

- "Lack of motivation. You will not learn unless you throw yourself in."

- "Dressing in a sloppy, unprofessional manner. Yes, there are times when blue jeans are sensible, but everything should be worn with a sense of style. I had one intern who went to a job site in a dress and heels. The workmen loved it of course since there were several levels to the unfinished house. The intern, however looked pretty dumb, and she was with me. Another intern and I spent a day on a job site during the summer. I had told her it would be okay to wear shorts, thinking of course, that they would be Bermuda shorts…but she showed up in shorts too short to be professional and we were meeting part of the way there, so there was no chance for her to change clothes."

- "Thinking that after a short time they are equipped to be an 'interior designer' and inability to listen."

- "Unreliability, lack of communication skills."

- "Lack of initiative, carelessness, and transition from college life to the real business world."

- "Attitude or thinking they are above a given task."

- "Someone who doesn't listen to project description or requirements."

- "They expect to have the same privileges as owners and hide from some jobs no one wants to do, i.e., filing new product info into it's proper place and not leaving the old price list in."

- "Not showing up on time."

- "Not having a work ethic."

- "Do not show up on time, don't take the work seriously, waste time, don't ask questions."

- "Interns with a perceived disinterest in the profession are perplexing and annoying. Interns who think they will be hired and suddenly be made the head designer need to understand there is so much more to the profession."

- "Not excited about helping with basic tasks, interns don't always take each task as a learning opportunity, but instead feel too good for certain jobs."

- "Personal cell phone calls and personal emailing and non-work related chats in the office. Also bringing personal problems to work."

- "Using our supplies for their personal use. Taking or receiving personal phone calls throughout the day either on our time or their personal cell phones. Not telling the truth is 'an out the door' for me. Chewing gum, perfume is not acceptable. Acting inappropriate with the client or the trades people. Not conducting themselves in a lady-like or gentlemanly manner. Taking stamps to be used for personal mail. Using computer for personal work, wasting time on the Internet that is not work related to the office. Bringing a lunch that smells up the office and the odor lingers all day, offending others. Annoying habits that should have been broken when they were two years old (trilling their hair when thinking, sucking thumb). Must have their own car to drive to work. Get to work on time and not depend on public transportation."

- "Interoffice chatting and petty jealousies. The employee that butters-up the boss is usually as transparent as glass. Constant cell phone calls from friends/boyfriends/kids/family and chat with them break up concentration and are a distraction."

- "Not able to function in the real world. Too timid and insecure."

- "Most design interns don't realize that what they are doing is equally important to the overall team effort. Sometimes they dawdle over things that should only take minutes and rush through things that are really important. Time is money. When tasks are given to them, the need to move through them as quickly and efficiently as possible."

- "Many don't take it seriously."

- "Unreliability, calling last minute to say that they have a midterm and can't make it to their intern shift."

- "Work on their portfolio on company time."

- "Those who do not take the opportunity seriously and do not work hard or learn. They cheat themselves as well as the employer."

81

- "Know-it-alls. Many interns think they can do or know more than they really do. Too much social chatting and slow or sloppy work. Someone who makes too many excuses."

- 'What can you do for me attitude."

As quoted by my father when we discussed intern attitudes, "The only job I know of where you can begin at the top is digging a hole." Do not expect to come in and be the head designer when you are an intern. It just does not work that way.

What an Employer Wants and Why They Hire

The best advice you can get on how to get hired is listed below. These quotes are from the ones who do the hiring. They have been candid and direct in telling you what makes you a "keeper". Want to get hired full-time or as an intern for that matter? Follow the advice they give you!

- "By working well with others, actually having a talent and an eye for design, but most of all having an interest to learn as we work on various projects through out their time with us."

- "A passion for design, cheerfulness, multitasking ability, competence in basic aspects of the design process, some basic classes or advanced, able to speak, write and read English."

- "Willingness to wear any of the necessary hats. We have all emptied the trash before a big client appointment or helped with lunches or coffee for a client."

- "Enthusiasm about the opportunity, willingness to do what it takes to get the job done regardless of title, self-motivator, organized."

- "Honesty, good work ethic, ability to support the team and add value to our work."

- "Having everything it takes including sale ability, great listening skills, organized, multi-tasker, able to delegate and manage others and self, very creative and innovative, loves people and can manage clients and projects at a very high level of expertise, many, many years before becoming a designer."

- "Go above and beyond what is expected. Be eager to learn and receptive to criticism, make yourself invaluable."

- "Know CAD, enthusiasm, and a willingness to work and contribute, knowledge of finishes and furniture, good attitude."

- "Knows what to do and answers questions accordingly. Asks intelligent questions. Looks and sounds the part of one of our employees. How well they fit in from a personality standpoint and work ethic perspective. Are they a go getter, self-starter?"

- "One who has an attitude to learn and can listen to instructions and can be self-directed when waiting for project work."

- "Punctuality, reliability, non-slacking on the job, no excessive office socializing, going the extra step on a job, ability to learn and perform, not making mistakes, thinking."

- "Hardworking, when they see a problem, they find a solution and bring to the employer. A lot of times employer realizes something isn't working properly but doesn't' have the time right away to come up with solutions. When solutions and choices are brought to them it makes their job easier."

- "The intern follows instructions and asks questions, doesn't act like a Prima Dona right out of school, is willing to take on any kind of task to be a useful team player."

- "Good attitude. Have an interest in all aspects of the profession. Be professional. Be on time and courteous. Treat the internship like a full-time job and not a way of passing time over the break."

- "Following directions, accuracy, professional manners, ability to learn quickly and learn on their own. Generally someone who makes it worth the employer's investment to stay on staff."

- "Good attitude for working, self-motivated, not always waiting to be told what to do, eager to learn and grow."

- "Eager to learn and pleasant to work with and the clients like them. I want them to work like it is their own company."

- "Being easy to have around and willing to tackle most any task. No attitude. Polite and gracious manner with clients. Being willing and able to work overtime on occasion."

- "Willing to do all sorts of tasks, from drafting to shopping to filing and phones. The more flexible and capable you are, the more trainable you are. The most important thing is a great attitude. Nothing can happen unless you have an open attitude towards learning and becoming part of a bigger team."

- "Talent and personality."

- "Make yourself invaluable."

- "Has earned trust from the designers on staff by following directions, being proactive and respectful, being reliable and resourceful, self-starter, proactive."

- "Ability to take a task to the next level or at least be as complete as possible."

- "Reliable, detail oriented, willing to work hard, confident, focused."

- "Hard work and a willingness to go the extra mile. Someone who works quickly and shows a dedication to our projects – which may mean working overtime to help meet deadlines. Be thorough and leave your attitude at the door."

- "Ask for things to do. Don't wait to be told what to do. Solving problems and taking initiative are the best ways to stand out from the crowd."

- "Make sure you have completed all your assigned tasks before leaving. If you didn't finish something make sure your manager knows why you were unable to complete the task."

- "Take initiative – if you are bored, tell someone."

- "Ask for things to do. Don't wait to be told what to do. Solving problems and taking initiative are the best ways to stand out from the crowd."

- "Be nice to everyone – many interns do not realize that gaining the respect of assistants, mail-room workers, and other support staff can be as important as winning the appreciation of executives. When it comes time to be considered for a full-time position, how you treat support staff can make a difference in whether you get a job offer."

- "Volunteer for extra assignments – during slow periods, be sure to track down your supervisor and volunteer for extra assignments, something few interns bother to do. The more initiative and enthusiasm you show, the more responsibility you will get."

- "Show up on time, be responsible, work hard and limit the amount of time you spend socializing. Doing so will go a long way toward proving your integrity and worth."

- "Employers love employees who dive into tackling tough problems and who think outside the box in finding solutions, however, there is a fine line between taking initiative and being perceived as a know it all……it is best to err on the side of caution."

While this chapter may seem to be nothing but lists of quotes, I felt it was important for students and future interns to read the actual quotes so they could see how many different designers mentioned the same issues, good and bad. They all seem to be dealing with the same problems when working with interns.

Now you know what employers in the design industry are looking for in a "keeper". While you cannot do everything during one semester, focus on the most important tips given. Take special notice of the ones mentioned in the majority of the replies. Adopting those character traits will lead you to success!

Chapter 6:
After the Internship

Your internship should have been more than just a semester away from campus or "just that thing you did during the summer". You should have increased your knowledge base during the experience, about yourself as well as the industry. Now that it is over, what is your next step?

There are several important steps you need to complete to keep your internship experience current in your mind. Answering the questions listed below in this post-internship checklist will help determine where you are now and what you need to do to move forward to the next phase of your career.

Take Stock of What You Learned

First, do you still want to work in the design industry? If you did not like the job duties, the field or industry as a whole, this would be the time to meet with a career counselor to discuss alternative areas in design or other options you might try.

If you enjoyed the work, what did you learn? Did you accomplish your goals or did you go above and beyond your expectations? What did you fail to accomplish? What was the most important thing you learned from this experience?

Did you learn anything about your organizational, work-related and design skills and abilities? What did you learn about yourself as you dealt with coworkers, supervisors, vendors and clients?

Have your career options expanded? Were you introduced to areas within the industry of which you were previously unaware? Has your network of contacts within the industry enlarged?

How did you like the work environment? Was the type of organization, location and atmosphere one you would seek after graduation? Why or why not? What skills, equipment or office technology did you master?

Making a list of the things you enjoyed and the things you want to avoid will help you during your search for employment. Write down what you have learned and think about how you want to describe your experience in interviews and on your resume'.

Build on the experience, as your internship should be a building block in your career. Look for ways to continue using what you learned as you move toward graduation or your first job.

Add New Skills to Your Resume

Update your resume' with the duties and responsibilities you had during your internship. Make note of job functions or areas of expertise you were exposed to through your observations.

If you need help in updating your resume', attend a resume'-writing workshop or ask your career counselor for assistance. Also, there are many resources available online, in the library or bookstore to guide you through creating a quality resume'.

Send Thank You Notes

Experts say most people underestimate the power of a handwritten thank you. Your effort in sending a thank you note, especially when handwritten, can wield considerable power and influence and reflects favorably on your character.

Write to your primary supervisor and thank them for helping make your internship experience a valuable one. Do more than just say "thanks" and sign it. Give specific reasons. Let them know how they assisted in your career development.

You might also send a note to other designers, architects or vendors you interacted with during your internship. They could be valuable contacts in the future, but make sure you are sincere and not just "throwing flowers".

Make sending the thank you note a high priority. It should be sent within three days of your last day as an intern. Handwritten notes sent by snail mail are the most effective way to show your appreciation.

Ask for a Recommendation

Before you leave, ask your supervisor for a letter of recommendation. Request the letter while you are there and still fresh in their mind as it may be harder to get after you leave.

If you forget, you may request a recommendation afterward via a follow-up note or phone call. Make the process easy for the writer by giving a list of points they might include such as your basic job duties, what you learned and how you excelled.

Be sure to send a thank you afterward, especially if they had to produce the letter quickly for you.

Keep in Touch

During your internship you may have had the opportunity to meet with many other professionals in the industry such as manufacturer's reps, architects, engineers, and contractors. Continuing to nurture these relationships is important, as these professionals also know what is going on with other companies and the industry in general. Reps are great resources for product information and continuing education.

If you are interested in returning for another internship or future employment, talk to your supervisor. Do not assume they know of your interest. If they liked having you, chances are they will ask you to return or offer you a position if one is available.

The Art of Networking

As a student, join and participate in local professional associations such as ASID, IIDA or IFDA. There is a high probability the people whom you worked with at the site will also be members. These are also great networking opportunities for you to meet others in the industry and provide additional support as you are searching for a job.

Joining professional networking groups on the Internet such as LinkedIn can connect you with classmates and colleagues extending your network of trusted contacts. Groups such as these can also be places to ask questions and receive advice from experienced professionals.

Chapter 7:
Final Words of Advice

To find the internship that is right for you, you will have to open your eyes and really scrutinize each company you research. There will be some trial and error. In the beginning, everyone puts their best foot forward so you will not observe some characteristics of a company until you have been there a while. Applying with companies you respect and admire for their high standards and goals that are similar to your own will big a key factor in finding the perfect internship for you.

An internship is a transition period, from youth to adulthood. Even though you will technically still be a student, you have just entered the professional world. Act like it. You will be working on real-life projects. Not only are thousands of dollars at stake, so is the livelihood of your co-workers. Your mistakes could cost the company money, reputation or even a client.

Remember your journey does not end with landing the right internship. Being hired as a full-time designer requires finding the right company AND getting your professional act together. It takes both of these steps to find an optimal work environment where you will thrive as an entry-level designer. Daily improvement of your skills and talents is important, but improvement of your personal characteristics, habits and traits is essential.

You stand on the threshold of the door to your future. Use the keys provided in this book to open the door to your dreams. If you read and study the material discussed in the previous chapters, you will be better prepared as a design student for your internships and subsequently become one of the best entry-level designers hired. Good luck!

Appendices

Appendix A:
Assessment Questions

These questions are taken from the text of the book and are listed here to assist you in your personal assessment.

How well do you do in the following areas?

Personality Traits –

- Cheerful, happy demeanor
- Always pleasant
- Friendly and gets along well with others
- Positive "can do" attitude
- Perseveres through difficulties
- Enthusiastic with high energy level
- Mature, responsible and dependable
- Honest and trustworthy
- Able to maintain confidences
- High standards and professional ethics
- Poised and confident

- Dedicated and committed
- Observant and inquisitive
- Flexible, versatile and open-minded
- Humble and thoughtful of others
- Does not gossip or speak negatively of others

Work ethic –

- Willing and eager to learn, teachable
- Willing to do anything, fearlessness, not shy or timid
- Willing to work hard
- Self-starter, go-getter, has initiative
- Able to multi-task
- Able to work with limited assistance
- Organized and prepared
- Accurate and attentive to details
- Able to focus, attentive to others when needed
- Interested in all aspects of profession, not just design
- Able to manage time efficiently, complete assignments quickly
- Reliable, punctual, dependable
- Not a clock watcher

Design Skills -

- Talented with passion for the profession
- Excellent color sense
- Good presentation skills and color board prep
- Good drawing and freehand sketching / illustration ability
- Good understanding of furniture and fabrics

- Good understanding of how to resource materials
- Able to think "outside the box"
- AutoCAD or REVIT, Studio IT, Photoshop familiarity

Office Skills –

- Good record keeping and organizational skills
- Office or retail experience
- Good telephone etiquette and language skills
- Good grammar and writing skills
- Familiar with basic office programs such as Word, Excel, etc.
- Computer hardware and software knowledge
- Excellent computer skills

People Skills –

- Well-mannered
- Good listener (incredibly important!)
- Good verbal communication
- Team player
- Easy speaking manner
- Problem solving skills
- Able to think on your feet

Ask yourself the following questions:

Personal -

- What can you offer an employer *right now*?
- What improvements do you need to make?

- How do you rate in dress and grooming?
- Do you have any clothing suitable for work in a design office?
- What kind of accessories are the norms?
- What are acceptable hairstyles?
- What about your physical appearance?
- Are you neat and clean?
- Do you have good hygiene?
- Do you always look like you just rolled out of bed?
- What does your posture say about you – enthusiastic or slacker?
- Are there skills you have or can develop to fill a need for a company?
- Did you accomplish your goals or did you go above and beyond your expectations?
- What did you fail to accomplish?
- What was the most important thing you learned from this experience?
- Did you learn anything about your organizational, work-related and design skills and abilities?
- What did you learn about yourself as you dealt with coworkers, supervisors, vendors and clients?

Intern Job -

- Does your school have specific internship requirements you need to meet prior to graduation?
- Do you want to learn a specific skill or just beef-up your resume?

- Do you need cash as an incentive or can you work for free or next to nothing?
- Do you want to work in an interior design firm or a design department within an architectural firm?
- Would you be interested in space planning for a furniture or kitchen showroom?
- What about interning with a design/build business?
- Have you thought of working within a design department of a large corporation or retail business?
- Do you want to intern locally or in another area?
- Do you want to do residential or commercial design?
- Are you interested in specialty areas such as healthcare, hospitality, corporate, retail or institutional design?
- Have you thought about government work?
- Do you eventually want to become a licensed professional?
- Now that it is over, what is your next step?
- Do you still want to work in the design industry?
- If you enjoyed the work, what did you learn?
- Have your career options expanded?
- Were you introduced to areas within the industry of which you were previously unaware?
- Has your network of contacts within the industry enlarged?
- How did you like the work environment?
- Which do you value most: flexibility, creativity or coworker interaction?

- Was the type of organization, location and atmosphere would seek after graduation? Why?
- What skills, equipment or office technology did you master?

Appendix B:
Meal Etiquette

While meal etiquette was not ranked high in importance in the survey replies, it is nonetheless important. If you look around you in restaurants, you will probably see many of the negatives listed below happening at each table, especially people eating with their mouth open.

The first priority of a business meal is business. Eating is secondary. Table manners are easily scrutinized and, unfortunately, too many people jeopardize the opportunity to build relationships when they fail to use proper dining etiquette.

So how do *you* rate? Will your conduct over a meal help or hurt your reputation? Will your guests be looking for a quick exit or will they have a pleasant experience and be glad to have met with you over lunch?

There are many books at the library and a great deal of information available online about etiquette in general. The information in this appendix is provided as a bonus to give you some basic rules, specifically regarding business meal etiquette.

Use this list of do's and don'ts to assess your knowledge of mealtime manners and adjust your habits so you make the best possible impression.

- If you are the host, take the least desirable seat (the one facing the wall, kitchen or restrooms) and let your guests have the prime seats (the ones with the view).

- Sit next to your guest at a right angle rather than across the table. If there are two guests, seat one across from you and one to your side rather than sitting between them (to avoid the ping-pong effect during conversation).

- If you know your guest well, you have a basis for small talk. If you do not know them well, spend time getting acquainted prior to beginning business.

- Small talk about sports, weather, and current events is good. Avoid talk of salary, benefits, problems, off-color jokes, gossip, religion or politics.

- If time is an issue, eliminate some of the chitchat. Keep your eye on the time, but do not let your guests see you checking your watch.

- If someone else is paying for the meal, show respect for his or her budget and order something in the middle price range on the menu.

- Allow your guests to order first and order as many courses as they do. It can be awkward if one orders an appetizer or dessert and the others do not and have to wait.

- Some foods are meant to be eaten with the fingers while some are meant to be eaten with a fork, so use care when ordering. Order foods that are familiar and easy to eat. Avoid foods like spaghetti, fried chicken, ribs and lobster.

- Unfold your napkin and place it in your lap shortly after you are seated. Keep it there unless you need to wipe something from your lips. If you leave your seat, place your napkin in a loose fold in your chair. After the meal, place the napkin to the side of your plate.

- Wait until everyone at your table is served before you begin eating. If your plate is the one still missing, encourage others to begin without you so their food doesn't get cold.

- Understand place settings:
  - Silverware will be arranged from the outside in.
  - Salad fork to the left of the dinner fork.
  - Dinner fork to the left of the plate.
  - Soup spoon/fruit spoon will be on the outside of the right side of the plate (if soup or fruit are served as a first course).
  - Dinner knife will be just to the right of the dinner plate, (used for entrée).
  - Butter knife will be placed across the edge of the bread plate.
  - Bread plate is just above the forks and slightly to the left
  - Dessert fork or spoon can be presented above the dinner plate at the beginning of the meal or the waiter might bring it to you.
  - More formal restaurants will have a service plate (a large plate on which another plate will be placed).

- The water glass is placed just above the knife.
- Coffee cup and saucer are to the right of the setting with spoon on the right side.
- If confused about which drink is yours, remember BMW – **B**read on the left, **M**eal in the middle, **W**ater on the right.

- Food is served from the left and drinks are served from the right.

- Bread is often the first food on the table and usually must be passed around. Put the butter on your bread and butter plate (and keep them there), then break (don't cut) the bread one bite at a time and butter each bite individually.

- Generally, pass items to your left and unless something is right in front of you, ask that it be passed to you.

- Cut enough food for one to two bites, eat it, and then cut one to two more.

- Wait until you taste your food before seasoning it.

- Place sweetener wrappers neatly next to your glass or under your saucer.

- Remember what your mother taught you – say please and thank you.

- Do not reach across someone for something at the table.

- **Never** talk with food in your mouth and keep your mouth closed when chewing.

- **Never** spit a bad piece of food into your napkin. Remove it from your mouth with your silverware and place on the edge of your plate.

- If food spills off your plate, use your fork to pick it up and place on the edge of your plate.

- For heaven's sake, **never** pick your teeth or use your napkin to blow your nose at the table! We should not have to mention this but do because we have seen it happen in restaurants.

- Keep the chair legs on the floor and your elbows off the table.

- Absolutely no grooming at the table! Excuse yourself and head to the restroom if you need to take care of something.

- DO NOT DRINK ALCOHOL even if it is offered.

- Turn your cell phone off! Answering a call tells your guests that you and your caller are more important – serious breach of etiquette. If you forget and it rings audibly, reject the call, apologize and turn off the ringer.

- If you are the host, you decide when to start discussing business so use good judgment. If you wait too long, your guests may begin to wonder why they were invited. If you start too early, they may feel you are more interested in their money than you are in them.

- Breakfast meals are short so get to business quickly. Discussions at lunch should wait until after you order to avoid being interrupted. Dinner allows more time to build rapport so limit business talk until after the main course is completed.

- Handle any disasters with poise and grace. If there are any problems with the restaurant, excuse yourself to discuss them with the staff. Do not complain in front of your guests.

- When you are finished with your meal, lay the knife and fork side by side in the center of your plate as a signal to your waiter you are finished. Do not push you plate out of the way when you are through.

- It is inappropriate to ask for a 'to-go' bag after a business meal.

- Do not fight over who pays the bill. If in doubt, pick up the check.

- Always make sure your guests know how much you appreciate their time and especially be sure to thank them if they pay for your meal.

Now that you know the basics, try a test meal using your family or friends as your guests. Work on your table manners so your social skills shine with sophistication!

Appendix C:
Ratings from the Surveys

Since some of you might be curious about the survey questions and where certain tasks rank in importance, I have included survey replies here.

Designers were asked to rank the following tasks. They are listed from most to least important.

Design Skills:

    1 - Illustration skills

    2 - Drafting / CAD skills

    3 - Presentation boards

    4 - Selection of finish materials

    5 - Selection of furnishings

    6 - Selection of fabric

Resourcing:

    1 - Use of library materials

2 - Working with manufacturer's reps

3 - How to resource on the Internet

4 - Organizing resource files

5 - Finding local resources

Personal Skills:

1 - Attitude / behavior

2 - Following directions

3 - Work habits / proper use of time

4 - Realistic expectations of the internship

5 - Common courtesy

6 - Telephone etiquette

7 - Ethics / honesty

8 - Confidentiality

9 - Interaction with co-workers

Those who hire ranked the following skills. Their replies are also listed from most to least important.

Work Skills:

1 - Attitude / behavior on the job

2 - Organizational skills

3 - Record keeping

4 - Proper use of time

5 - Quality of portfolio

6 - Quality of resume'

7 - Telephone manners

8 - Interview skills

9 - Internet / email use

10 - Meal etiquette

Personal Traits:

1 - Listening / following directions

2 - Honesty / ethics

3 - Ability to work with others

4 - Promptness

5 - Self-starter ability

6 - Confidentiality

7 - Common courtesy

8 - Proper dress for work

9 - Conflict resolution

10 - Office politics

It is interesting to note both designers and those who hire rank attitude, behavior, listening and following directions at the top of the list. Again, while all listed are important skills and traits, start your self-improvement with the ones at the top of each list.

Appendix D:
Helpful Information

Interior Design Links

www.InteriorDesignJobs.com

--Jobs specific to interiors

www.ASID.org

--Job bank listings

www.IIDA.org

--Career Center job listings

www.NKBA.org

--Keyword search - Internships

www.i-d-d.com

--Directory of designers listed by state

www.Indeed.com

--Directory of job listings from major job boards, newspapers, associations and company career pages, updated daily. Keyword search for interior design intern.

General Internship Links

www.MonsterTrak.com

—Top college oriented job-listing database and also houses an internship database.

www.InternWeb.com

--Has an advanced search feature that enables you to specify location, industry, job function, time of year and keyword. Requires you to register but it is free.

www.InternJobs.com

--Can search specifically for interior design jobs

www.Job-e-Job.com

--Has specific search for interior design intern jobs

www.design-engine.com

--Job postings for many 'design' fields – Interior design is one category available to search.

Self Improvement Books – a few of the best!

- How to Win Friends and Influence People by Dale Carnegie

- 100 Absolutely Unbreakable Laws of Business Success by Brian Tracy

- The Success Principles: How to Get from Where You Are to Where You Want to Be by Jack Canfield

- Think and Grow Rich by Napoleon Hill

- The Seven Habits of Highly Effective People by Stephen R. Covey

About the Author

During her years of experience in commercial design, Jeanette H. Simpson, ASID has hired, trained and mentored many new employees. Drawing from this and her own experience transitioning from design student to employee, comes *From Interior Design Intern to Employee: How to Be a "Keeper" (Including Tips from Those Who Hire)*.

Jeanette is the founder and president of KidSpace Interiors, located in Lakewood Ranch, Florida where she provides commercial and residential design for children's spaces. Before opening KidSpace, Jeanette worked for architectural firms in Atlanta, Georgia and Sarasota, Florida where she was part of award winning design teams.

As a professional member of ASID, an NCIDQ Certificate holder and a licensed designer in Florida, she has worked in many segments of the interior design industry. Project areas include hospitality, corporate, medical, retail, residential and kitchen design.

Jeanette holds a Bachelor of Arts degree in Interior Environment from Brigham Young University in Provo, Utah. As a mother of six, stepmother of five and grandmother of eleven (and counting), she has plenty of experience in training children, youth and young adults to have a strong work ethic and be successful employees.

She is also a furniture designer for a fine children's furniture company located in Santa Ana, California. Her in-depth understanding of parents' needs and children's wants strengthens her abilities in designing for children.

Other published works include design related articles that can be found on eHow.com.

Made in the USA
San Bernardino, CA
22 July 2017